ARCTIC OCEAN

NORTH AMERICA

ATLANTIC OCEAN

PACIFIC OCEAN

SOUTH AMERICA

Managing editor Sophie Amen Managing art editor and cartographer Bruno Douin Translation into English Miranda Smith Editor Jill Anderson

The surface of our planet is made up of
large areas of land · the continents ·
surrounded by lots and lots of water.

THE OCEANS

Four huge oceans · the Pacific, the Atlantic, the Indian
and the Arctic · as well as many seas, cover almost
three-quarters of the surface of the Earth.
The Pacific is the largest of the oceans. The Arctic Ocean is
quite different from the others · it is at the North Pole ·
and is almost always covered with a thick layer
of ice called an ice shelf.

THE CONTINENTS

The seven continents are Africa, North America, South America, Asia, Europe,
Australia, and Antarctica.

Only Antarctica, at the South Pole, is not home to people. It is entirely
covered with ice and is so cold that people cannot live there.

The other six continents are divided into countries. The borders, or edges, of
these countries are shown on the tracing pages of this book. Some borders
follow the course of a river or a chain of mountains, but not always. Some
borders have been decided by wars, and others are still being fought over.

MY FIRST TRIP AROUND THE WORLD

EDITOR'S NOTE

All the political and physical maps in this atlas are faithful to reality,
although they have been simplified to make them easier to read.
However, on the big illustrations that guide the reader across the
different continents, the illustrators have deliberately distorted
the distances and the scale to give the young reader a richer view of the world.

We hope you have a good trip!

TWO CAN

CHANHASSEN, MINNESOTA · LONDON

AFRICA

Africa is a land of contrasts. The Sahara Desert covers the northern one-third of the continent. Farther south, the grassy savanna gives way to thick forests. Small villages and modern cities are often close neighbors.

In the old streets of Marrakech, in Morocco, the market, or souk, is very lively. Sellers and buyers argue over prices, while others relax with a glass of mint tea.

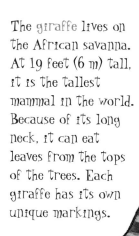

The giraffe lives on the African savanna. At 19 feet (6 m) tall, it is the tallest mammal in the world. Because of its long neck, it can eat leaves from the tops of the trees. Each giraffe has its own unique markings.

Just outside the large towns and cities of South Africa are areas called townships that are home mostly to poor black Africans. Soweto, outside Johannesburg, is one of the poorest of these townships.

One of Africa's famous landmarks is Mount Kilimanjaro, an active volcano. Its snow-covered peak towers over the savanna, a wide area covered with tall grasses.

The Djenné Mosque, in Mali, is built entirely from mud bricks that were dried in the sun. Its spiky appearance comes from pieces of wood that stick out of the mud. Muslims come from near and far to pray at this holy site.

In Zimbabwe, the women of the Ndebeles tribe are nicknamed "giraffe women" because their necklaces make their necks look very long.

Members of the Pygmy tribe are less than 5 feet (1.5 m) tall. They live just as they did thousands of years ago, hunting animals and gathering berries and fruits in the thick forests near the equator.

The baobab tree survives the dry season because it stores water in its trunk. Legend says that the tree was planted upside down, with its roots in the sky.

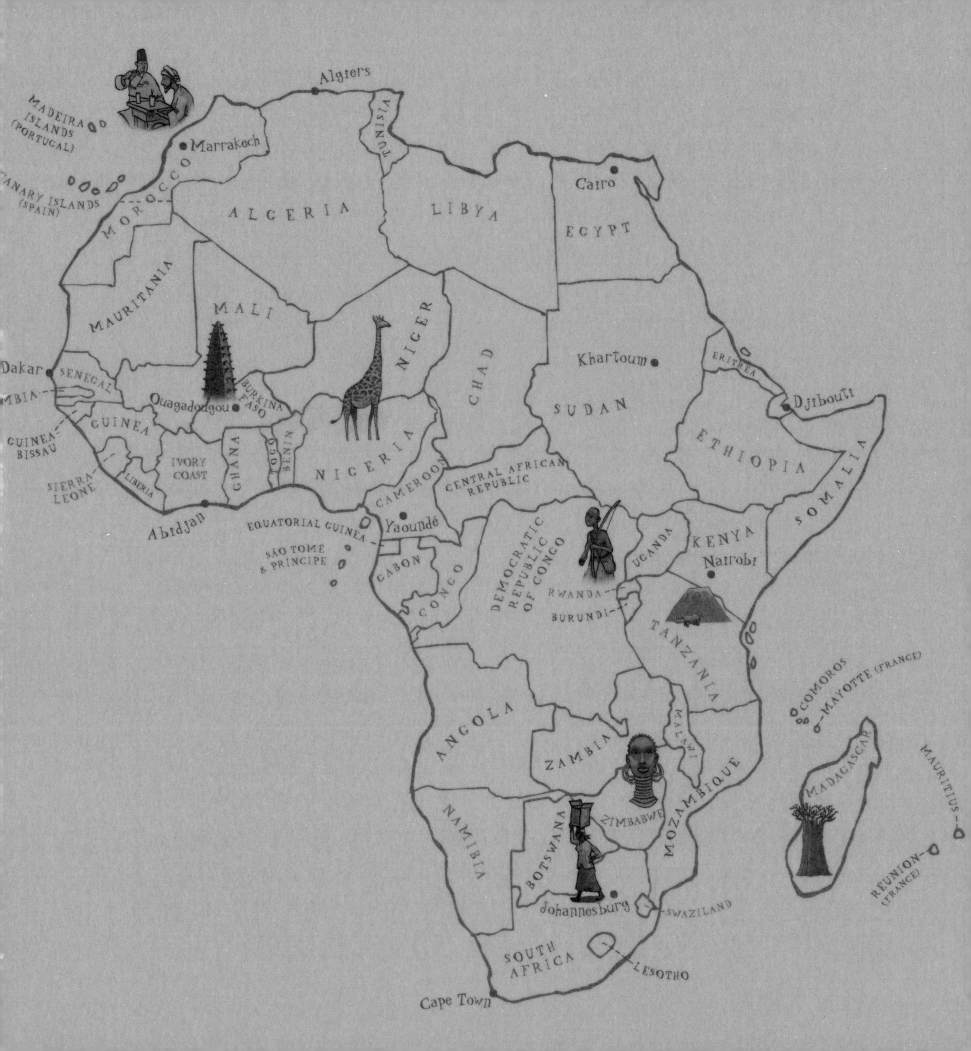

MADEIRA ISLANDS (PORTUGAL)

Algiers

CANARY ISLANDS (SPAIN)

MOROCCO

Marrakech

ALGERIA

TUNISIA

LIBYA

Cairo

EGYPT

MAURITANIA

MALI

NIGER

CHAD

SUDAN

Khartoum

ERITREA

Djibouti

Dakar

SENEGAL

GAMBIA

GUINEA-BISSAU

GUINEA

Ouagadougou

BURKINA FASO

ETHIOPIA

SOMALIA

SIERRA LEONE

LIBERIA

IVORY COAST

GHANA

TOGO

BENIN

NIGERIA

CAMEROON

CENTRAL AFRICAN REPUBLIC

Abidjan

EQUATORIAL GUINEA

Yaoundé

SÃO TOMÉ & PRÍNCIPE

GABON

CONGO

DEMOCRATIC REPUBLIC OF CONGO

RWANDA

BURUNDI

UGANDA

KENYA

Nairobi

TANZANIA

COMOROS

MAYOTTE (FRANCE)

ANGOLA

ZAMBIA

MALAWI

MOZAMBIQUE

MADAGASCAR

MAURITIUS

NAMIBIA

BOTSWANA

ZIMBABWE

Johannesburg

SWAZILAND

RÉUNION (FRANCE)

SOUTH AFRICA

LESOTHO

Cape Town

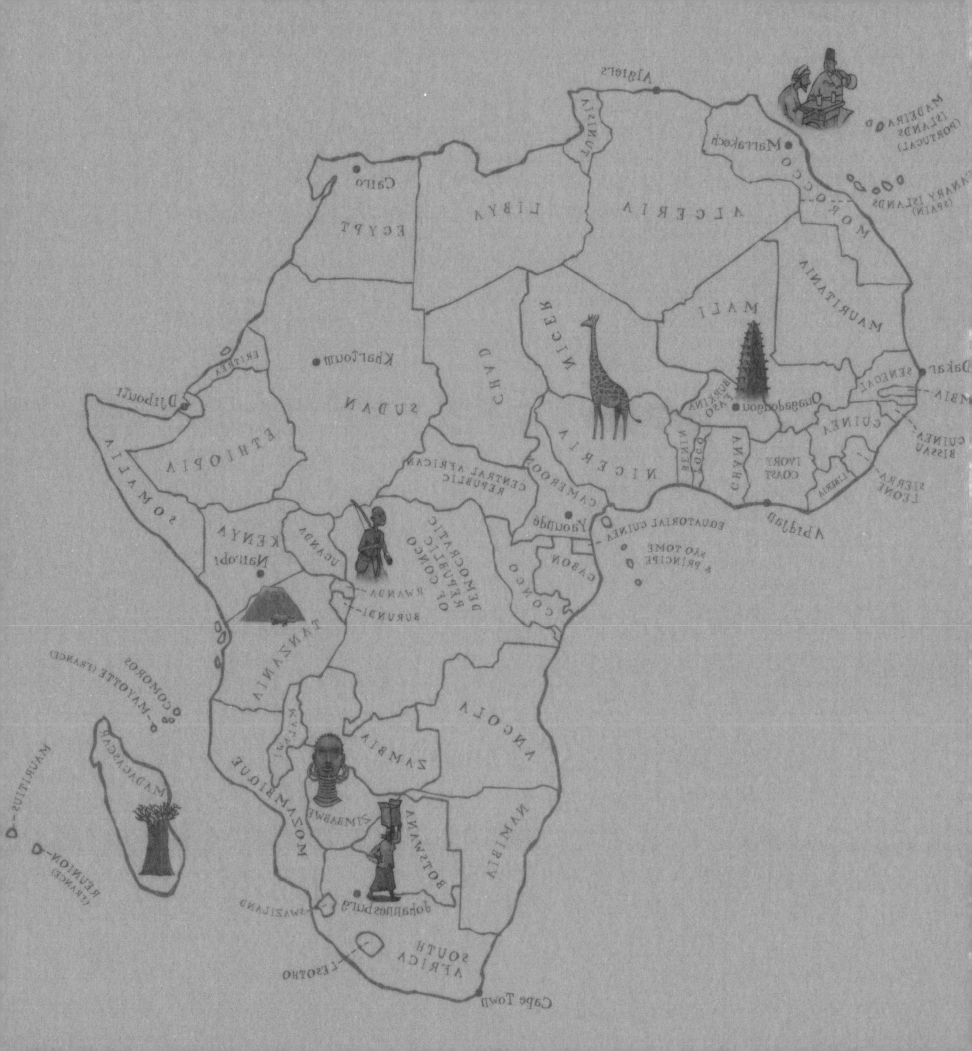

ATLAS MOUNTAINS

Mediterranean Sea

LIBYAN DESERT

Suez Canal

Red Sea

S A H A R A   D E S E R T

SAHEL

Niger

Lake Chad

Nile

Nile

GREAT RIFT VALLEY

Lake Victoria

Mount Kilimanjaro

Gulf of Guinea

Congo

Lake Tanganyika

Lake Malawi

ATLANTIC OCEAN

INDIAN OCEAN

Zambezi

KALAHARI DESERT

NORTH
WEST   EAST
SOUTH

Cape of Good Hope

IN AFRICA, YOU CAN CRUISE THE NILE

The River Nile flows from Lake Victoria north to the Mediterranean Sea. It goes through the tropical forests of Uganda and the deserts of Sudan and Egypt. There are countless villages on its banks. The Nile has supported the people that live there since the pharaohs ruled as gods over Egypt.

Sinai Peninsula

Suez Canal

Red Sea

CAIRO

the god Amun

Temple of Karnak

the goddess Mut

Temple of Luxor

Nile

Aswan Dam

Nile delta

Pyramids

Lake Nasser

Temple of Edfou

Mediterranean Sea

Sphinx of Giza

felucca

the god Horus

sarcophagus

archaeological site

Egyptian cat

belly dancer

Ra   Thoth   Osiris   Sobek

In the time of the pharaohs, the gods of ancient Egypt were always pictured with the heads of sacred animals.

ALEXANDRIA

oil wells

Tuareg caravan

EAST

NORTH

SOUTH

WEST

Mount
Kenya

zebra

pride of lions

safari
in
Kenya

elephants

Temple of
Philae

palm grove

Khartoum
Mosque

leopard

Nile

crocodiles

pink
flamingos

Temple of
Abu Simbel

cheetah

antelope

white
pelican

zebu

zebra

date
palm

Sudanese
village

Jackal

rhinoceros and young

gorilla and
young

equatorial
forest

NORTH AMERICA

Three large countries – Canada, the United States, and Mexico – make up most of North America. The smaller countries south and east of Mexico are sometimes called Central America.

Large areas of Canada and the U.S. are wilderness. Raccoons often can be found near running water.

The beaver is an excellent swimmer. With its strong teeth, this tubby architect cuts down large trees. It eats the bark and uses the branches to build its dams.

The Statue of Liberty watches over the entrance to the port of New York, the largest city in the United States. The statue was given to the United States by France in 1876. She has seen millions of immigrants arrive since then, all dreaming of life in a new world.

Towering over the jungle in Guatemala, the pyramid of Tikal is 230 feet (70 m) high. It was built around 500 by the Maya, an advanced civilization that has since died out.

The Inuit people live mostly in the far north. When they go on seal or whale hunts, they build shelters called igloos from blocks of ice. They catch fish by making holes in the ice.

Cuba is the largest of the islands in the Caribbean. Many Cubans have a passion for music. Day and night, the rhythms of drums called congas fill the streets of Havana.

The polar bear lives near the North Pole, in the Arctic. Its thick fur coat protects it from the cold. It is a strong swimmer and a clever seal hunter. Special pads on its paws keep it from slipping on the ice.

On the Canada-United States border, the spectacular Niagara Falls attract thousands of tourists a year. They wear rain gear to stay dry in the misty air.

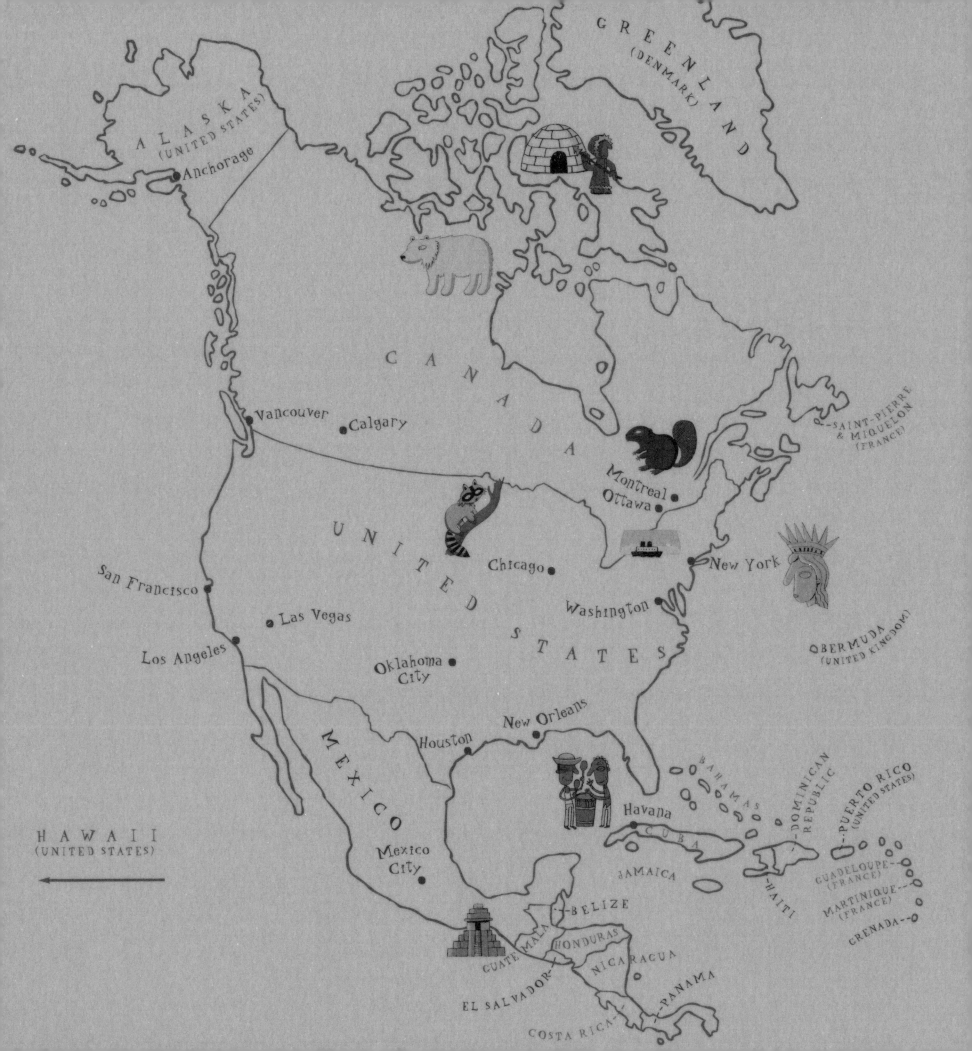

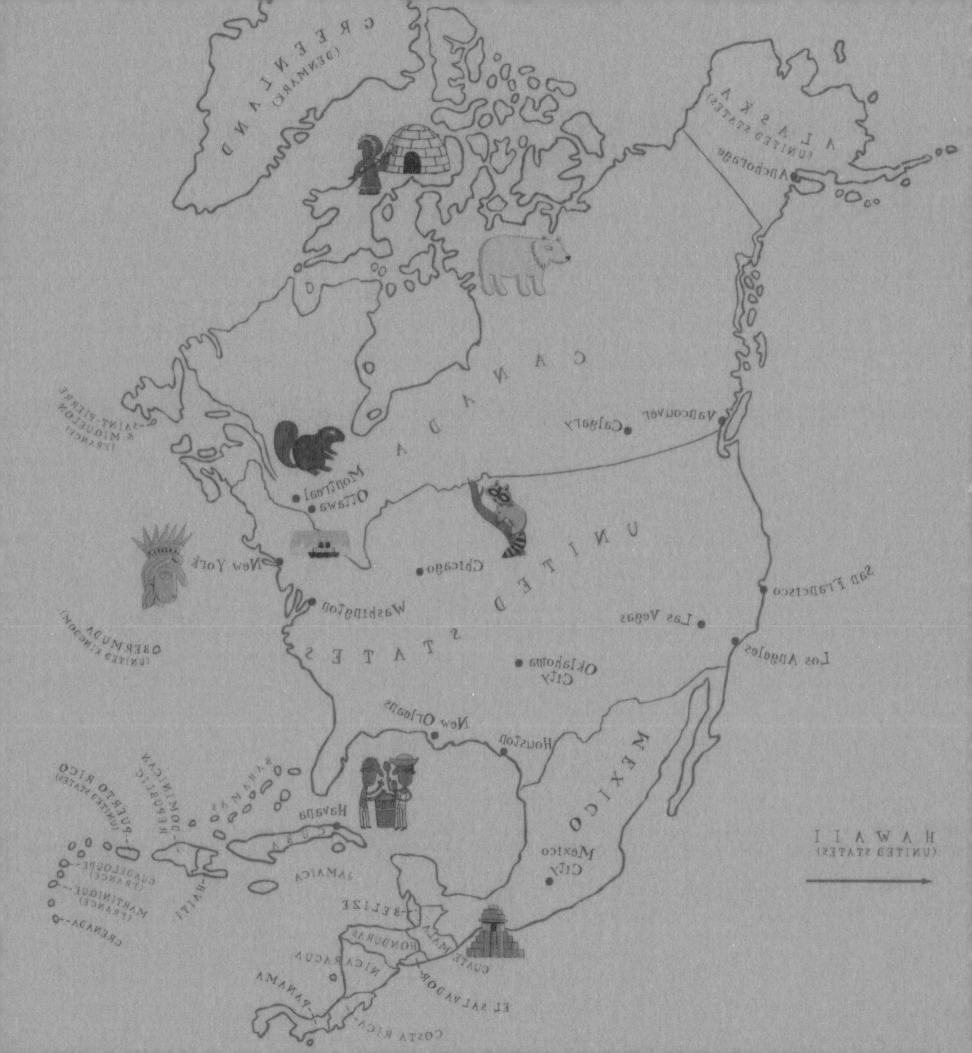

SOUTH AMERICA

The country of Brazil covers nearly half the South American continent. Brazil is home to the largest forest in the world: the Amazon rain forest.

Once a year, people from all over the world arrive in Rio de Janeiro, in Brazil, to celebrate carnival. The crowds dress up and parade along the streets, dancing among brightly colored floats.

The city of Kourou, on the coast of French Guiana, is home to a large space center where rockets are launched.

The toucan lives in the hot, humid rain forest. This magnificent bird is in danger of extinction.

Lake Titicaca is the highest navigable lake in the world. It has dozens of floating islands on it that are made out of reeds. The native Uro people use reeds to build their houses, their beds, and their boats.

Located in southeastern Brazil, São Paulo is the largest city in South America. Some of its residents live in run-down neighborhoods called favelas.

A mighty river, the Amazon, flows through the rain forest. Nicknamed "the green lungs of the world," the rain forest shelters several native tribes, thousands of colorful birds and insects, many wild animals, and towering trees.

Caracas

VENEZUELA

TRINIDAD AND
TOBAGO

Bogotá

COLOMBIA

GUYANA

SURINAME

Kourou

FRENCH
GUIANA

ECUADOR

PERU

BRAZIL

Lima

La Paz

Brasília

BOLIVIA

PARAGUAY

Rio de Janeiro

São Paulo

URUGUAY

Santiago

ARGENTINA

CHILE

Buenos Aires

Montevideo

FALKLAND ISLANDS
(UNITED KINGDOM)

Ushuaia

IN SOUTH AMERICA, YOU CAN VISIT THE ANDES

The Andes is the longest mountain chain in the world. Stretching 5,000 miles (8,000 km) down the west side of the continent, the range passes through some very different climates: hot and humid areas in the north, fertile pastures of the pampas in the center, and the desert plateau of Patagonia in the south.

PACIFIC OCEAN

Easter Island

Mount Aconcagua

Atacama Desert

fur seal

llama

Perito Moreno glacier

gauchos

penguins

Ushuaia

BUENOS AIRES

oil wells

albatross

wheat fields

Biscay whales

Falkland Islands

ATLANTIC OCEAN

ASIA

Asia is the largest of the continents. It has more people than any other continent.

For thousands of years the Mongols were nomads, or wanderers. Most still live in tents called yurts, which are easy to take down and carry around. The Mongols drive their goats and sheep over the dry grasslands of Mongolia.

The giant panda lives in the forests and mountains of China. Bamboo is its only food. Now this plant is slowly disappearing, and the panda is in danger of dying out.

The Taj Mahal, in the Indian city of Agra, is one of the most beautiful monuments in the world. Built of white marble, it is a tomb built by an emperor after his beloved wife died.

The Newars live in Nepal, at the foot of the Himalayas, the highest chain of mountains in the world. The Newars have built many Hindu temples, which are famous for their stacked roofs.

Buddhism is a religion from southeast Asia and Tibet that has spread across the world. It is a religion that seeks out wisdom. Its founder, Buddha, was a prince who gave up all his possessions so that he could meditate and live a simpler life.

The Great Wall of China was built in the 3rd century BC. The wall, which is more than 1,800 miles (3,000 km) long, protected China from enemy attacks.

For centuries, people in southern Asia hunted the Bengal tiger for its fur. Now there are few of these beautiful creatures left.

R U S S I A

TURKEY

CYPRUS

LEBANON-
ISRAEL-
alem

JORDAN

SAUDI ARABIA

KUWAIT

BAHRAIN-

QATAR-

UNITED
ARAB EMIRATES

ecca

YEMEN

OMAN

GEORGIA

AZERBAIJAN

ARMENIA

SYRIA

Baghdad

IRAQ

IRAN

Tehran

KAZAKHSTAN

UZBEKISTAN

TURKMENISTAN

AFGHANISTAN

Kabul

PAKISTAN

KYRGYZSTAN

TAJIKISTAN

MONGOLIA

C H I N A

Beijing

Vladivostok

NORTH
KOREA

SOUTH
KOREA

JAPAN

Tokyo

Shanghai

TAIWAN

New
Delhi

Kathmandu

NEPAL

Lhasa

BHUTAN

Agra

I N D I A

Calcutta

BANGLADESH

MYANMAR

Hanoi

LAOS

THAILAND

Bombay

CAMBODIA

VIETNAM

Manila

PHILIPPINES

BRUNEI

SRI LANKA

MALAYSIA

SINGAPORE

MALAYSIA

MALDIVES

I N D O N E S I A

Jakarta

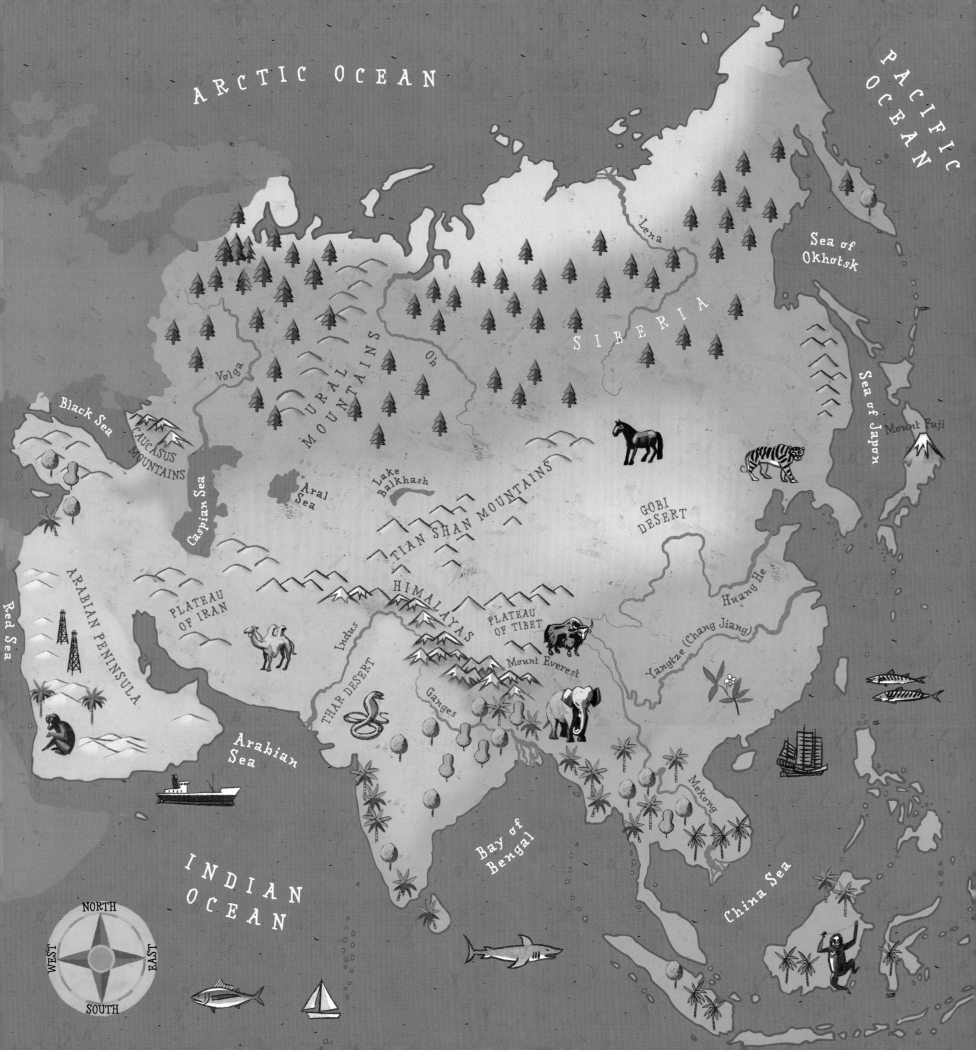

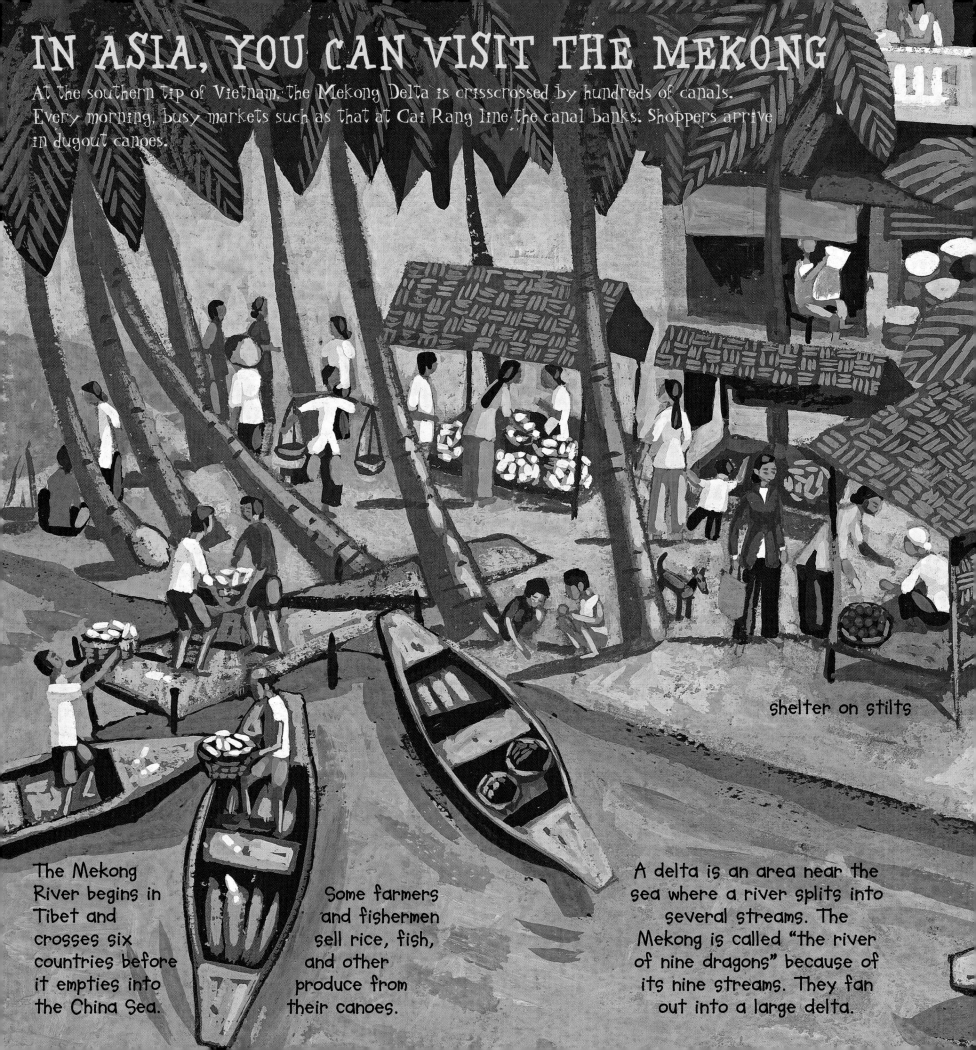

IN ASIA, YOU CAN VISIT THE MEKONG

At the southern tip of Vietnam, the Mekong Delta is crisscrossed by hundreds of canals.
Every morning, busy markets such as that at Cai Rang line the canal banks. Shoppers arrive
in dugout canoes.

shelter on stilts

The Mekong
River begins in
Tibet and
crosses six
countries before
it empties into
the China Sea.

Some farmers
and fishermen
sell rice, fish,
and other
produce from
their canoes.

A delta is an area near the
sea where a river splits into
several streams. The
Mekong is called "the river
of nine dragons" because of
its nine streams. They fan
out into a large delta.

temple

incense

yoke

rickshaw

The rickshaw is a popular way to travel in Asian towns and cities.

Half of all the rice grown in Vietnam comes from the Mekong Delta.

A yoke is a long pole with a basket attached at either end.

EUROPE

Europe is the smallest continent on the planet, but one where many people live. It is a continent that has many different countries, languages, and cultures.

In France, 37 species of cow are bred for their meat or milk. Many wonderful cheeses are made there.

The town of Amsterdam, in the Netherlands, has many canals. Paths along the canals are perfect for the many people who travel by bicycle.

Under the Spanish sun, a bullfight is about to begin. Bull and matador face each other. With his muleta, or cape, the matador teases the bull until it charges. Then he tries to get out of the way. The crowds cheer for their favorite.

The fjords, on the west coast of Norway, are valleys that were carved out by glaciers and then filled with sea water. They are steep, winding waterways that are often very deep.

St. Basil's Cathedral in Moscow is one of the masterpieces of Russian architecture. It was built in the 16th century on the orders of the czar, or ruler, Ivan the Terrible. He had the architect blinded so that he could never again build anything so beautiful.

White houses and churches with blue roofs dot the landscape of Hydra, one of the Greek islands. Cars are not allowed here. The locals travel by scooter or donkey. Boats bring food and supplies when the sea is calm.

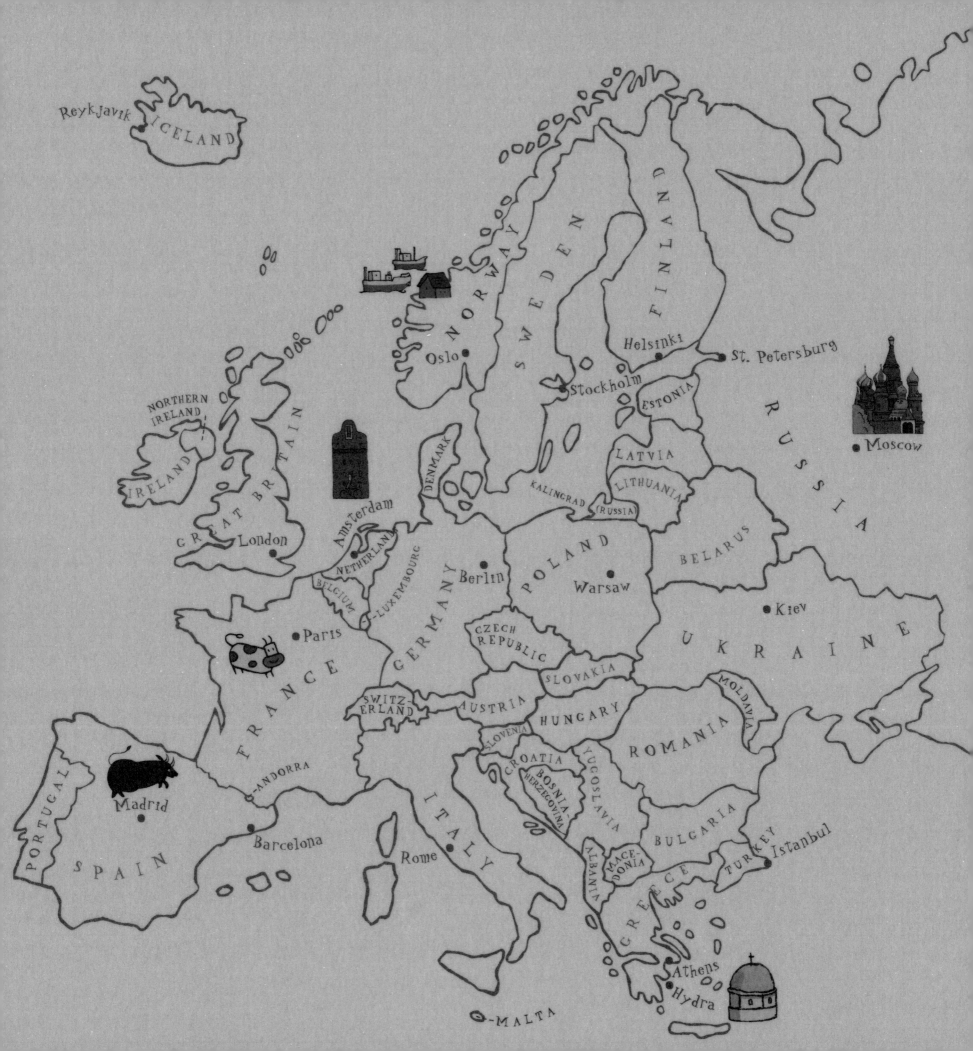

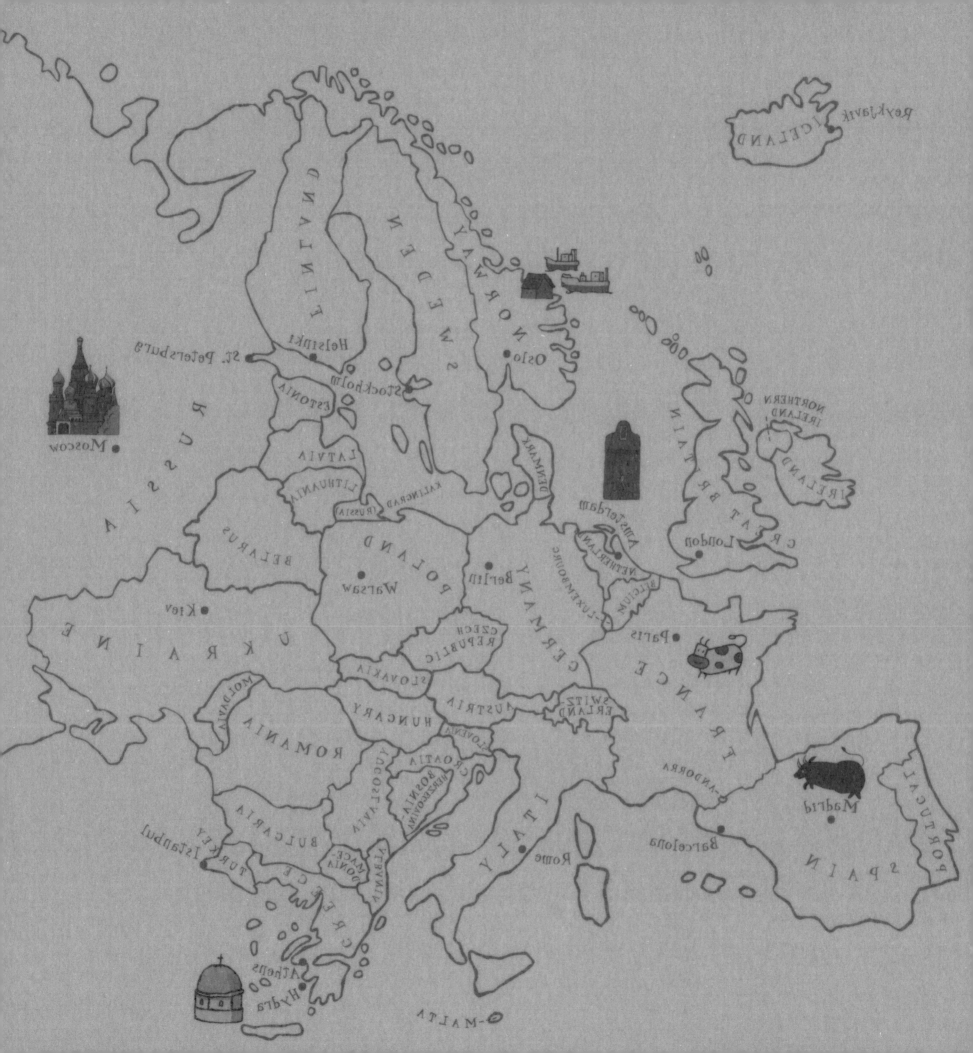

IN EUROPE, YOU CAN RIDE THE ORIENT EXPRESS

The Orient Express is a luxury train that carries famous people across Europe. It is featured in many books and films. The journey begins in England, winds through France, Switzerland, and Austria, and ends in Italy.

AUSTRALIA

Blue as far as the eye can see, this area of the South Pacific is made up of thousands of islands, friendly people, some unusual wildlife, and lots of sunshine.

The Great Barrier Reef is over 1,200 miles (2,000 km) long. Every day, tiny marine creatures called polyps add to its length. To protect themselves, they make a sort of rocky shelter called coral. Corals come in all shapes and colors.

Sydney is the largest city in Australia. It is a port, located on one of the most beautiful bays in the world. It is famous for its opera hall, which looks like a group of sailboats at the water's edge.

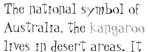

The national symbol of Australia, the kangaroo lives in desert areas. It can jump huge distances because of its strong back legs.

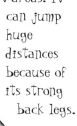

The island of New Guinea is a really wild place. The native Papuans live in houses on stilts 165 feet (50 m) above the ground. They try to live in harmony with nature.

From a very young age, children in New Zealand play rugby at school. The All Blacks rugby team, with its eye-catching black jerseys, is one of the best in the world.

Ayers Rock, in the Australian desert, is the largest rock in the world. It is sacred to the native Aborigines, who consider it to be a living being named "Uluru."

The farmers of the Australian Outback look after millions of sheep using motorbikes or helicopters. The area is so vast and the farms are so isolated that children do their schooling by radio.

With its white petals and delicate smell, the gardenia is the symbol of the South Pacific. People of Tahiti twist the flowers into necklaces for tourists.

MIDWAY ISLANDS
(UNITED STATES)
HAWAII
(UNITED STATES)
Honolulu
NORTHERN MARIANAS
(UNITED STATES)
JOHNSTON ATOLL
(UNITED STATES)
GUAM
(UNITED STATES)
MARSHALL ISLANDS
MICRONESIA
NAURU
KIRIBATI
PAPUA NEW GUINEA
SOLOMON ISLANDS
TUVALU
TOKELAU
(NEW ZEALAND)
WALLIS & FUTUNA ISLANDS
(FRANCE)
SAMOA
COOK ISLANDS
(NEW ZEALAND)
FRENCH POLYNESIA
Papeete
VANUATU
FIJI
Suva
TONGA
NEW CALEDONIA
(FRANCE)
Nouméa
Alice Springs
AUSTRALIA
Perth
Sydney
Auckland
NEW ZEALAND

HAWAII
(UNITED STATES)
Honolulu

MIDWAY ISLANDS
(UNITED STATES)

JOHNSTON ATOLL
(UNITED STATES)

NORTHERN MARIANAS
(UNITED STATES)

GUAM
(UNITED STATES)

MICRONESIA

MARSHALL
ISLANDS

KIRIBATI

NAURU

TUVALU

TOKELAU
(NEW ZEALAND)

WALLIS & FUTUNA
ISLANDS
(FRANCE)

SAMOA

FIJI   Suva

VANUATU

SOLOMON ISLANDS

PAPUA NEW
GUINEA

FRENCH
POLYNESIA
Papeete

COOK ISLANDS
(NEW ZEALAND)

TONGA

NEW
CALEDONIA
(FRANCE)   Nouméa

AUSTRALIA

Alice Springs

Sydney

Perth

NEW ZEALAND
Auckland

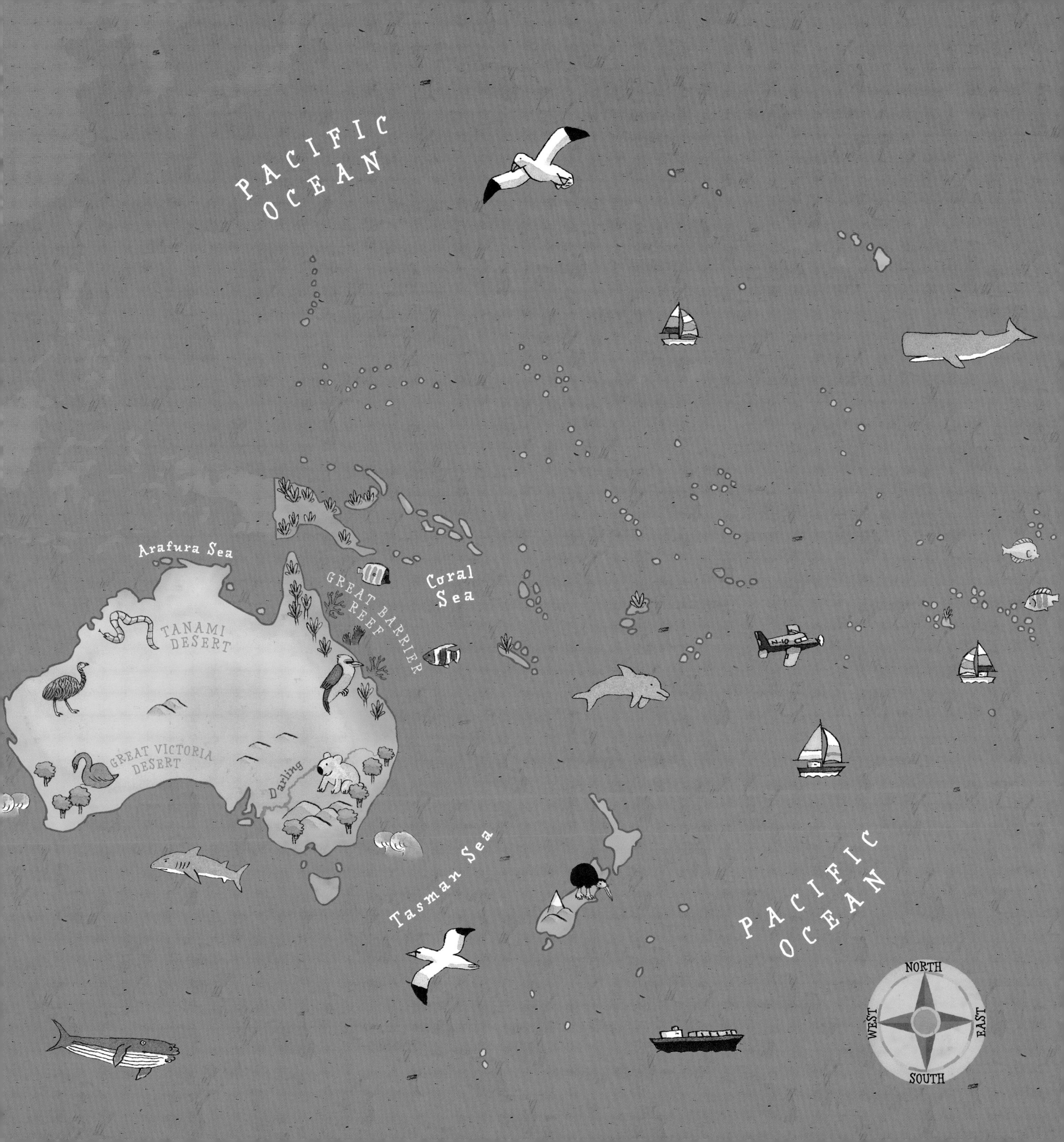

PACIFIC
OCEAN

Arafura Sea

Coral
Sea

GREAT BARRIER REEF

TANAMI
DESERT

GREAT VICTORIA
DESERT

Darling

Tasman Sea

PACIFIC
OCEAN

N-10

NORTH
WEST   EAST
SOUTH

IN AUSTRALIA, YOU CAN VISIT AN ATOLL

Among the islands now known as French Polynesia lies an ancient, underwater volcano.
Corals attached themselves to the rim of the volcano and built it up until it formed a ring
above the water's surface – the Rangiroa atoll.

airport

coconut grove

manta ray

fishing
with nets
and
spears

surgeon fish

coral

water
reservoir

traditional
village

dugout canoe

sea turtle

humpback
whale

islet

luxury
hotel

houses on stilts

clownfish

butterfly fish

bread tree

school

dancers

truck

coconut crab

traveler's tree

banana
plantation

PACIFIC
OCEAN

shark

dolphin

Europe was illustrated by Olivier Latyk...

...Asia by Marcelino Truong...

...Africa by Florent Silloray...

...Australia by François Roudot.

Published in 2004 by Two-Can Publishing
an imprint of Creative Publishing international, Inc.
18705 Lake Drive East
Chanhassen, MN 55317
1-800-328-3895
www.two-canpublishing.com

Original edition published in French under
the title of "Mon premier tour du monde"
© 2002 Edition MILAN.
300 rue Léon Joulin, 31101 Toulouse cedex 9 · France

English text copyright © Two-Can Publishing

ISBN 1-58728-515-0

Library of Congress Cataloging-in-Publication data: pending

1 2 3 4 5 6 09 08 07 06 05 04

Printed in Italy